Baking

Everyday recipes to enjoy

chocolate fudge cake

ingredients

SERVES 8

175 g/6 oz unsalted butter,
    softened, plus extra
    for greasing
175 g/6 oz golden caster sugar
3 eggs, beaten
3 tbsp golden syrup
40 g/1^1/$_2$ oz ground almonds
175 g/6 oz self-raising flour
pinch of salt
40 g/1^1/$_2$ oz cocoa powder

icing

225 g/8 oz plain chocolate,
    broken into pieces
55 g/2 oz dark muscovado
    sugar
225 g/8 oz unsalted butter,
    diced
5 tbsp evaporated milk
^{1}/$_2$ tsp vanilla extract

method

1 Grease and line the bottom of 2 x 20-cm/ 8-inch round cake tins. To make the icing, place the chocolate, sugar, butter, evaporated milk and vanilla extract in a heavy-based pan. Heat gently, stirring constantly, until melted. Pour into a bowl and cool. Cover and chill in the refrigerator for 1 hour, or until spreadable.

2 Place the butter and sugar in a bowl and beat together until light and fluffy. Gradually beat in the eggs. Stir in the syrup and ground almonds. Sift the flour, salt and cocoa into a separate bowl, then fold into the mixture. Add a little water, if necessary, to make a dropping consistency. Spoon the mixture into the prepared tins and bake in a preheated oven, 180°C/350°F/Gas Mark 4, for 30–35 minutes, or until springy to the touch and a skewer inserted in the centre comes out clean.

3 Leave the cakes in the tins for 5 minutes, then turn out onto wire racks to cool completely. When the cakes are cold, sandwich them together with half the icing. Spread the remaining icing over the top and sides of the cake, swirling it to give a frosted appearance.

carrot cake

ingredients

MAKES 16 PIECES

2 eggs

175 g/6 oz molasses sugar

200 ml/7 fl oz sunflower oil

200 g/7 oz coarsely grated
    carrots

225 g/8 oz wholemeal flour

1 tsp baking soda

2 tsp ground cinnamon

whole nutmeg, grated
    (about 1 tsp)

115 g/4 oz roughly chopped
    walnuts

topping

115 g/4 oz half-fat
    cream cheese

4 tbsp butter, softened

85 g/3 oz icing sugar

1 tsp grated lemon rind

1 tsp grated orange rind

method

1 In a mixing bowl, beat the eggs until well blended and add the sugar and oil. Mix well. Add the grated carrot, sift in the flour, baking soda and spices, then add the walnuts. Mix everything together until well incorporated.

2 Grease and line a 20-cm/8-inch round cake tin. Spread the mixture into the prepared cake tin and bake in the centre of a preheated oven, 190°C/375°F/Gas Mark 5, for 40–50 minutes until the cake is nicely risen, firm to the touch and has begun to shrink away slightly from the edges of the tin. Remove from the oven and cool in the tin until just warm, then turn out onto a wire rack to cool completely.

3 To make the topping, put all the ingredients into a mixing bowl and beat together for 2–3 minutes until really smooth.

4 When the cake is completely cold, spread with the topping, smooth over with a fork, and allow to firm up a little before cutting into 16 portions. Store in an airtight container in a cool place for up to one week.

blueberry & lemon drizzle cake

ingredients

SERVES 12

225 g/8 oz butter, softened,
  plus extra for greasing
225 g/8 oz golden caster
  sugar
4 eggs, beaten
250 g/9 oz self-raising flour,
  sifted
finely grated rind and juice
  of 1 lemon
25 g/1 oz ground almonds
200 g/7 oz fresh blueberries

topping

juice of 2 lemons
115 g/4 oz golden caster
  sugar

method

1 Grease and line the bottom of a 20-cm/ 8-inch square cake tin. Place the butter and sugar in a bowl and beat together until light and fluffy. Gradually beat in the eggs, adding a little flour towards the end to prevent curdling. Beat in the lemon rind, then fold in the remaining flour and almonds with enough of the lemon juice to achieve a good dropping consistency.

2 Fold in three-quarters of the blueberries and turn into the prepared tin. Smooth the surface, then scatter the remaining blueberries on top. Bake in a preheated oven, 180°C/350°F/ Gas Mark 4, for 1 hour, or until firm to the touch and a skewer inserted into the centre comes out clean.

3 To make the topping, place the lemon juice and sugar in a bowl and mix together. As soon as the cake comes out of the oven, prick it all over with a fine skewer and pour over the lemon mixture. Cool in the tin until completely cold, then cut into 12 squares to serve.

gingerbread

ingredients

MAKES 12–16 PIECES

450 g/1 lb plain flour

3 tsp baking powder

1 tsp baking soda

3 tsp ground ginger

175 g/6 oz butter

175 g/6 oz soft brown sugar

175 g/6 oz black molasses

175 g/6 oz golden syrup

1 egg, beaten

300 ml/10 fl oz milk

method

1 Line a 23-cm/9-inch square cake tin, 5 cm/2 inches deep, with baking paper.

2 Sift the flour, baking powder, baking soda and ginger into a large mixing bowl.

3 Place the butter, sugar, molasses and syrup in a medium pan and heat over a low heat until the butter has melted and the sugar dissolved. Leave to cool a little.

4 Mix the beaten egg with the milk and add to the cooled syrup mixture. Add the liquid ingredients to the flour mixture and beat well using a wooden spoon until the mixture is smooth and glossy.

5 Pour the mixture into the prepared tin and bake in the centre of a preheated oven, 160°C/325°F/Gas Mark 3, for $1^{1}/2$ hours until well risen and just firm to the touch.

6 Remove from the oven and cool in the tin. Once cool, remove the cake from the tin with the lining paper. Wrap with foil and store in an airtight container for up to one week to allow the flavours to mature. Cut into wedges to serve.

devil's food cakes with chocolate icing

ingredients

MAKES 18

3 1/2 tbsp soft margarine

115 g/4 oz brown sugar

2 large eggs

115 g/4 oz plain flour

1/2 tsp baking soda

25 g/1 oz cocoa powder

125 ml/4 fl oz soured cream

icing

125 g/4 1/2 oz plain chocolate

2 tbsp caster sugar

150 ml/5 fl oz soured cream

chocolate curls

100 g/3 1/2 oz plain chocolate
(optional)

method

1 Put 18 paper baking cases in a muffin tin, or put 18 double-layer paper cases on a baking sheet.

2 Put the margarine, sugar, eggs, flour, baking soda and cocoa in a large bowl and, using an electric hand whisk, beat together until just smooth. Using a metal spoon, fold in the soured cream. Spoon the batter into the paper cases.

3 Bake the cupcakes in a preheated oven, 180°C/350°F/Gas Mark 4, for 20 minutes, or until well risen and firm to the touch. Transfer to a wire rack to cool.

4 To make the icing, break the chocolate into a heatproof bowl. Set the bowl over a pan of gently simmering water and heat until melted, stirring occasionally. Remove from the heat and cool slightly, then whisk in the sugar and soured cream until combined. Spread the icing over the tops of the cupcakes and allow to set in the refrigerator before serving. If liked, serve decorated with chocolate curls made by shaving plain chocolate with a potato peeler.

fruit & nut squares

ingredients

MAKES 9

115 g/4 oz unsalted butter,
   plus extra for greasing

2 tbsp honey

1 egg, beaten

85 g/3 oz ground almonds

115 g/4 oz no-soak dried
   apricots, finely chopped

55 g/2 oz dried cherries

55 g/2 oz toasted chopped
   hazelnuts

25 g/1 oz sesame seeds

85 g/3 oz rolled oats

method

1 Lightly grease an 18-cm/7-inch shallow, square baking tin with butter. Beat the remaining butter with the honey in a bowl until creamy, then beat in the egg with the almonds.

2 Add the remaining ingredients and mix together. Press into the prepared tin, ensuring that the mixture is firmly packed, and smooth the surface.

3 Bake in a preheated oven, 180°C/350°F/ Gas Mark 4, for 20–25 minutes, or until firm to the touch and golden brown.

4 Remove from the oven and let stand for 10 minutes before marking into squares. Cool completely before removing from the tin. Cut into squares and store in an airtight container.

peach cobbler

ingredients

SERVES 4–6

filling

6 peaches, peeled and sliced

4 tbsp caster sugar

$^1/_2$ tbsp lemon juice

$1^1/_2$ tsp cornflour

$^1/_2$ tsp almond or vanilla extract

vanilla or pecan ice cream,
    to serve

topping

175 g/6 oz plain flour

115 g/4 oz caster sugar

$1^1/_2$ tsp baking powder

$^1/_2$ tsp salt

85 g/3 oz butter, diced

1 egg

5–6 tbsp milk

method

1 Place the peaches in a 23-cm/9-inch square ovenproof dish that is also suitable for serving. Add the sugar, lemon juice, cornflour and almond extract and toss together. Bake the peaches in a preheated oven, 220°C/425°F/ Gas Mark 7, for 20 minutes.

2 Meanwhile, to make the topping, sift the flour, all but 2 tablespoons of the sugar, the baking powder and salt into a bowl. Rub in the butter with your fingertips until the mixture resembles breadcrumbs. Mix the egg and 5 tablespoons of the milk in a jug, then mix into the dry ingredients with a fork until a soft, sticky dough forms. If the dough seems too dry, stir in the extra tablespoon of milk.

3 Reduce the oven temperature to 200°C/ 400°F/Gas Mark 6. Remove the peaches from the oven and drop spoonfuls of the topping over the surface, without smoothing. Sprinkle with the remaining sugar, return to the oven and bake for a further 15 minutes, or until the topping is golden brown and firm – the topping will spread as it cooks. Serve hot or at room temperature with ice cream.

mississippi mud pie

ingredients

SERVES 8

pastry

225 g/8 oz plain flour,
    plus extra for dusting
2 tbsp cocoa powder
150 g/5^1/$_2$ oz butter
2 tbsp caster sugar
1–2 tbsp cold water

filling

175 g/6 oz butter
350 g/12 oz brown sugar
4 eggs, lightly beaten
4 tbsp cocoa powder, sifted
150 g/5^1/$_2$ oz plain chocolate
300 ml/10 fl oz single cream
1 tsp chocolate extract

to decorate

425 ml/15 fl oz double cream,
    whipped
chocolate flakes and curls

method

1 To make the pastry, sift the flour and cocoa powder into a mixing bowl. Rub in the butter with your fingertips until the mixture resembles fine breadcrumbs. Stir in the sugar and enough cold water to mix to a soft dough. Wrap the dough and chill in the refrigerator for 15 minutes.

2 Roll out the dough on a lightly floured work surface and use to line a 23-cm/9-inch loose-based tart tin or ceramic pie dish. Line with baking paper and fill with dried beans. Bake in a preheated oven, 190°C/375°F/Gas Mark 5, for 15 minutes. Remove from the oven and take out the paper and beans. Bake the pastry case for a further 10 minutes.

3 To make the filling, beat the butter and sugar together in a bowl and gradually beat in the eggs with the cocoa. Melt the chocolate and beat it into the mixture with the single cream and the chocolate extract.

4 Reduce the oven temperature to 160°C/325°F/Gas Mark 3. Pour the mixture into the pastry case and bake for 45 minutes, or until the filling has set gently.

5 Cool the mud pie completely, then transfer it to a serving plate, if you like. Cover with the whipped cream. Decorate the pie with chocolate flakes and curls and then chill until ready to serve.

almond tart

ingredients

SERVES 8

pastry

280 g/10 oz plain flour,
   plus extra for dusting
150 g/5^1/$_2$ oz caster sugar
1 tsp finely grated lemon rind
pinch of salt
150 g/5^1/$_2$ oz unsalted butter,
   chilled and cut into
   small dice
1 medium egg, beaten lightly
1 tbsp chilled water

filling

175 g/6 oz unsalted butter,
   at room temperature
175 g/6 oz caster sugar
3 large eggs
175 g/6 oz finely
   ground almonds
2 tsp plain flour
1 tbsp finely grated orange rind
^{1}/$_2$ tsp almond extract
icing sugar, to decorate
soured cream, to serve
   (optional)

method

1 To make the pastry, put the flour, sugar, lemon rind and salt in a bowl. Rub or cut in the butter until the mixture resembles fine breadcrumbs. Combine the egg and water, then slowly pour into the flour, stirring with a fork until a coarse mass forms. Shape into a ball and chill for at least 1 hour.

2 Roll out the pastry on a lightly floured work surface until 3 mm/^{1}/$_8$ inch thick. Use to line a greased 25-cm/10-inch tart tin. Return to the refrigerator for 15 minutes, then cover the pastry case with foil and fill with dried beans. Place in a preheated oven, 220°C/ 425°F/Gas Mark 7, and bake for 12 minutes. Remove the dried beans and foil and return the pastry case to the oven for 4 minutes. Remove from the oven and reduce the oven temperature to 200°C/400°F/Gas Mark 6.

3 Meanwhile, make the filling. Beat the butter and sugar until creamy. Beat in the eggs, one at a time. Add the almonds, flour, orange rind and almond extract and beat until blended.

4 Spoon the filling into the pastry case and smooth the surface. Bake for 30–35 minutes until the top is golden and the tip of a knife inserted in the centre comes out clean. Cool completely on a wire rack, then dust with sifted icing sugar. Serve with a spoonful of soured cream, if using.

date & honey loaf

ingredients

SERVES 10

butter, for greasing

250 g/9 oz strong white bread
    flour, plus extra for dusting

75 g/2³/₄ oz strong brown
    bread flour

¹/₂ tsp salt

1 sachet easy-blend dried
    yeast

200 ml/7 fl oz lukewarm water

3 tbsp corn oil

3 tbsp honey

75 g/2³/₄ oz dried dates,
    chopped

2 tbsp sesame seeds

method

1 Grease a 900-g/2-lb loaf tin with butter. Sift the white and brown flours into a large bowl and stir in the salt and yeast. Pour in the water, oil and honey and mix to form a dough.

2 Place the dough on a lightly floured work surface and knead for 5 minutes, or until smooth, then place in a greased bowl. Cover and let rise in a warm place for 1 hour, or until doubled in size.

3 Knead in the dates and the sesame seeds. Shape the dough and place in the prepared loaf tin. Cover and let stand in a warm place for a further 30 minutes, or until springy to the touch.

4 Bake the loaf in a preheated oven, 220°C/425°F/Gas Mark 7, for 30 minutes, or until the bottom of the loaf sounds hollow when tapped. Transfer to a wire rack and cool completely. Serve cut into thick slices.

apricot & walnut bread

ingredients

SERVES 12

55 g/2 oz butter, plus extra
   for greasing
350 g/12 oz strong white
   bread flour, plus extra
   for dusting
$1/2$ tsp salt
1 tsp golden caster sugar
2 tsp easy-blend dried yeast
115 g/4 oz no-soak dried
   apricots, chopped
55 g/2 oz chopped walnuts
150 ml/5 fl oz tepid milk
75 ml/$2^1/2$ fl oz tepid water
1 egg, beaten
vegetable oil, for brushing

topping

85 g/3 oz icing sugar
walnut halves

method

1 Grease and flour a baking sheet. Sift the flour and salt into a warmed bowl and stir in the sugar and yeast. Rub in the butter and add the chopped apricots and walnuts. Make a well in the centre. In a separate bowl, mix together the milk, water and egg. Pour into the dry ingredients and mix to a soft dough. Turn out onto a floured work surface and knead for 10 minutes, or until smooth. Place the dough in a clean bowl brushed with oil, cover with oiled clingfilm and let stand in a warm place for 2–3 hours, or until doubled in size.

2 Turn the dough out onto a floured work surface and knead lightly for 1 minute. Divide into 5 equal pieces and roll each piece into a rope 30 cm/12 inches long. Braid three ropes together, pinching the ends to seal, and place on the prepared baking sheet. Twist the remaining two ropes together and place on top. Cover lightly with oiled clingfilm and let stand in a warm place for 1–2 hours, or until doubled in size.

3 Bake the bread in a preheated oven, 220°C/425°F/Gas Mark 7, for 10 minutes, then reduce the heat to 190°C/375°F/Gas Mark 5 and bake for a further 20 minutes. Transfer to a wire rack to cool. To make the topping, sift the icing sugar into a bowl, stir in enough water to make a thin icing and drizzle over the loaf. Decorate with walnuts.

crusty white bread

ingredients

MAKES 1 MEDIUM LOAF

1 egg

1 egg yolk

tepid water, as required

500 g/1 lb 2 oz white bread
    flour, plus extra for dusting

1^1/$_2$ tsp salt

2 tsp sugar

1 tsp easy-blend dried yeast

2 tbsp butter, diced

vegetable oil, for brushing

method

1 Place the egg and egg yolk in a jug and beat lightly to mix. Add enough tepid water to make up to 300 ml/10 fl oz. Stir well.

2 Place the flour, salt, sugar and yeast in a large bowl. Add the butter and rub it in with your fingertips until the mixture resembles breadcrumbs. Make a well in the centre, add the egg mixture and work to a smooth dough.

3 Turn the dough out onto a lightly floured work surface and knead for 10 minutes, or until the dough is smooth and elastic. Place the dough in an oiled bowl, cover with clingfilm and leave in a warm place to rise for 1 hour, or until it has doubled in size.

4 Oil a 900-g/2-lb loaf tin. Turn the dough out onto a lightly floured work surface and knead for 1 minute until smooth. Shape the dough the length of the tin and three times the width. Fold the dough into three lengthways and place it in the tin with the join underneath. Cover and leave in a warm place for 30 minutes until it has risen above the tin.

5 Bake in a preheated oven, 220°C/425°F/ Gas Mark 7, for 30 minutes, or until firm and golden brown. Test that the loaf is cooked by tapping it on the bottom – it should sound hollow. Transfer to a wire rack to cool completely.

olive & sun-dried tomato bread

ingredients

SERVES 4

400 g/14 oz plain flour,
    plus extra for dusting

1 tsp salt

1 sachet easy-blend dried
    yeast

1 tsp brown sugar

1 tbsp chopped fresh thyme

200 ml/7 fl oz warm water
    (heated to 50°C/122°F)

4 tbsp olive oil, plus
    extra for oiling

50 g/1^3/$_4$ oz black olives,
    pitted and sliced

50 g/1^3/$_4$ oz green olives,
    pitted and sliced

100 g/3^1/$_2$ oz sun-dried
    tomatoes in oil, drained
    and sliced

1 egg yolk, beaten

method

1 Place the flour, salt and yeast in a bowl and mix together, then stir in the sugar and thyme. Make a well in the centre. Slowly stir in enough water and oil to make a dough. Mix in the olives and sun-dried tomatoes. Knead the dough for 5 minutes, then form it into a ball. Brush a bowl with oil, add the dough and cover with clingfilm. Let rise in a warm place for about 1^1/$_2$ hours, or until the dough has doubled in size.

2 Dust a baking sheet with flour. Knead the dough lightly, then cut into two halves and shape into ovals or circles. Place them on the baking sheet, cover with clingfilm and let rise again in a warm place for 45 minutes, or until they have doubled in size.

3 Make three shallow diagonal cuts on the top of each piece of dough. Brush with the egg. Bake in a preheated oven, 200°C/400°F/ Gas Mark 6, for 40 minutes, or until cooked through – they should be golden on top and sound hollow when tapped on the bottom. Transfer to wire racks to cool. Store in an airtight container for up to 3 days.

cheese & chive plait

ingredients

SERVES10

450 g/1 lb strong white bread
    flour, plus extra for dusting

1 tsp salt

1 tsp caster sugar

1½ tsp easy-blend dried
    yeast

2 tbsp butter

115 g/4 oz coarsely grated
    Cheddar cheese

3 tbsp snipped fresh chives

4 spring onions, chopped

150 ml/5 fl oz tepid milk

175 ml/6 fl oz tepid water

vegetable oil, for brushing

beaten egg, for glazing

method

1 Sift the flour and salt into a warmed bowl and stir in the sugar and yeast. Rub in the butter, then stir in the cheese, chives and spring onions. Make a well in the centre. Mix together the milk and water, pour into the well and mix to make a soft dough. Turn the dough out onto a lightly floured work surface and knead for 10 minutes, or until smooth and elastic.

2 Transfer the dough to a clean, oiled bowl and cover with clingfilm. Let stand in a warm place for 1 hour, or until doubled in size. Brush a large baking sheet with oil. Turn the dough out onto a floured work surface and knead for 1 minute. Divide the dough into three pieces. Roll out each piece into a rope shape and plait the three pieces together, pinching the ends to seal.

3 Place on the prepared baking sheet and cover with oiled clingfilm. Let stand in a warm place for 45 minutes, or until doubled in size. Brush with beaten egg and bake in a preheated oven, 220°C/425°F/Gas Mark 7, for 20 minutes.

4 Reduce the oven temperature to 180°C/350°F/Gas Mark 4 and bake for a further 15 minutes, or until golden brown and the loaf sounds hollow when tapped on the bottom. Serve warm or cold.

herb muffins with smoked cheese

ingredients

MAKES 12

1 tbsp sunflower or peanut
    oil, for greasing (if using)
280 g/10 oz plain flour
2 tsp baking powder
$1/2$ tsp baking soda
25 g/1 oz smoked hard
    cheese, grated
50 g/1$3/4$ oz fresh parsley,
    finely chopped
1 large egg, lightly beaten
300 ml/10 fl oz thick strained
    plain yogurt
4 tbsp butter, melted

method

1 Grease a 12-cup muffin tin with sunflower oil, or line it with 12 muffin cases. Sift the flour, baking powder and baking soda into a large mixing bowl. Add the smoked cheese and the parsley and mix together well.

2 In a separate bowl, lightly mix the egg, yogurt and melted butter together. Add the yogurt mixture to the flour mixture and then gently stir together until just combined. Do not overstir the batter – it is fine for it to be a little lumpy.

3 Divide the muffin batter evenly between the 12 cups in the muffin tin or the paper liners (they should be about two-thirds full), then transfer to a preheated oven at 200°C/400°F/ Gas Mark 6. Bake for 20 minutes, or until risen and golden. Remove the muffins from the oven and serve warm, or place them on a wire rack to cool.

This edition published by Parragon Books Ltd in 2013
LOVE FOOD is an imprint of Parragon Books Ltd

Parragon Books Ltd
Chartist House
15–17 Trim Street
Bath BA1 1HA, UK
www.parragon.com/lovefood

ISBN 978-1-4723-2233-3

Printed in China

Notes for the Reader

This book uses both metric and imperial measurements. Follow the same units of measurement throughout; do not mix metric and imperial. All spoon measurements are level: teaspoons are assumed to be 5 ml, and tablespoons are assumed to be 15 ml. Unless otherwise stated, milk is assumed to be full fat, eggs and individual vegetables are medium, and pepper is freshly ground black pepper. Unless otherwise stated, all root vegetables should be washed in plain water and peeled prior to using.

Garnishes, decorations and serving suggestions are all optional and not necessarily included in the recipe ingredients or method.

The times given are an approximate guide only. Preparation times differ according to the techniques used by different people and the cooking times may also vary from those given. Optional ingredients, variations or serving suggestions have not been included in the time calculations.

Recipes using raw or very lightly cooked eggs should be avoided by infants, the elderly, pregnant women, convalescents and anyone suffering from an illness. Pregnant and breastfeeding women are advised to avoid eating peanuts and peanut products. Sufferers from nut allergies should be aware that some of the ready-made ingredients used in the recipes in this book may contain nuts. Always check the packaging before use.